ARE YOU CERTAIN THAT YOU ARE GOING TO HEAVEN?

The Bible Says You Can Be!

"These things I have written to you….
so that you may know that you have eternal life."
I John 5:13

To Lori,
Someone who cares about others

Daniel Glenn Donahue

ISBN: 9781790977352

Scriptures – NASB

NOTE: Much of this book is taken from my book "Beyond Coincidence: Things in My Life That Only God Could Do," and Discipleship Evangelism, a ministry my wife Nancy and I were involved in for 33 years.

This is dedicated to my daughter Amy

and Her husband Wesley.

They are two very godly people,

who love God with all their hearts.

I'm very proud of them.

FORWARD

This book is written for people who don't know if they are going to heaven.

It is also written for those think they are going to heaven based on error.

How can you know for certain? How do you know where you will spend eternity? The Bible explains how you can know for certain.

TABLE OF CONTENTS

PART ONE

The Good News

Being Certain About Eternal Life

"These things I have written to you …. so that you may know that you have eternal life" (I John 5:13).

CHAPTER 1

WHERE WILL YOU SPEND ETERNITY?

HOW TO BE 100% WHERE YOU WILL GO WHEN YOU DIE

How can you know where you will spend eternity? First, I want to ask two very important questions that we all need to ponder. Ask yourself these questions before you read further. Write down your answers. The answers have eternal consequences.

DO YOU KNOW FOR CERTAIN THAT YOU ARE GOING TO HEAVEN?

We can be certain! The Bible says, **"These things I have written to you, so that you may know that you have eternal life."** *(1 John 5:13).* So, the Bible is telling us that we can know for certain if we will spend eternity with God in heaven or not.

HOW WOULD YOU ANSWER GOD IF HE ASKED YOU, *"WHY SHOULD I LET YOU INTO MY HEAVEN?"*

If you would like to know for certain why God would let you into heaven, and since the Bible tells us that we can know for certain, let's look at what the Bible tells us about eternal life. The answers might not be what you think.

GRACE

Here is an easier question than the first two. What is a free-gift? If you had to pay for something or received something because you earned it, would it be a free-gift?

If I reached out to you with my watch in my left hand and say, "I would like to give you my watch as a gift," and then, reach out with the right hand open and say, "that will be $375," what would you think? You would be asking me "what kind of gift is that?" If you had to pay for something, it's not free! If you got something because you earned it, it's not a free. If you got something because you deserved it, it's not a free-gift.

NOW, WHAT IF I TOLD YOU THAT HEAVEN IS A FREE-GIFT?

The Bible says, ***"For it is by grace you have been saved, through faith—and this is not from yourselves, it is the gift of God—not by works, so that no one can boast."*** *(Eph. 2:8-9)*. Let's examine this verse carefully.

So, if we are saved by ***"grace,"*** it must be important! So, what is grace? Grace is God freely giving us what we don't deserve.

Then, the verse says that we are saved ***"through faith."*** We will discuss that later.

HEAVEN IS NOT EARNED OR DESERVED

Notice then that the verse goes on to say ***"and this is not from yourselves, it is the gift of God—not by works, so that no one can boast."*** See, heaven is a ***"gift of God."*** If we could get to heaven by our own good works, then we could boast about ourselves and what we did to get into heaven. But ***"no one can boast "***about receiving a gift that they didn't earn or deserve.

So, if the nature of a gift, is that you can't pay for it or it's not a gift anymore - it's the same way with God's offer of the free-gift of heaven; you can't earn it; you can't do anything to get it.

The Bible also says, ***"not by works of righteousness which we have done, but according to his mercy he saved us"*** *(Titus 3:5)***.** This verse is saying that we are not saved by doing good things, but because of God's mercy. What is mercy? Mercy is like the flip side of grace. Remember,

"Grace" is God freely giving us what we don't deserve. "Mercy" is God not giving us what we do deserve.

But, even though heaven is a free-gift - not everyone is going to heaven. So, what determines who gets the free-gift of heaven and who doesn't? Let's look at why we don't deserve heaven and couldn't earn it if we tried.

MAN

MAN IS A SINNER

The Bible tells us that man is a sinner. Did you ever consider what sin is? Let's look at sin to expand our understanding of it.

There are sins where we do things that we shouldn't do, like murder, theft, lying, cheating, etc. Those are the things we think about most as being sin.

Not doing things that we should do is also sin! Did you realize that if someone needs help and you can help them, but you don't, it's a sin?

There are sins of thought. In the Sermon on the Mount, Jesus said that if you are angry with someone, you've committed murder in your heart *(Matt. 5:22)*. If you've lusted after someone, you've committed adultery in your heart *(Matt. 5:28).* He said calling someone a fool is a sin worthy of hell *(Matt 5:22).*

That is why the Bible teaches that all men are sinners. It says, ***"for all have sinned and fall short of the glory of God"*** *(Rom 3:23).* The Bible also says ***"indeed, there is not a righteous man on earth who continually does good and who never sins"*** *(Ecc. 7:20).* These verses say that everyone is a sinner? Why is that?

MAN CANNOT SAVE HIMSELF

Now, there is no sin in God and there is no sin in heaven, and the Bible says that if we commit one sin in our whole life, we might as well have committed them all *(James 2:10).* That's because the punishment is the same. It's not that getting angry with someone is as bad as killing them. It's the fact that no matter what the sin is, it will separate us from a perfect, holy God in Whom there is no sin. Think of it this way - if you commit one murder, you are a murderer! So, if you commit one sin you are a sinner!

So, how could anyone ever get to heaven? Yet, we know that many will. Let's look at God to understand why.

GOD

GOD IS LOVING AND MERCIFUL

God is loving and merciful, therefore, He doesn't want to punish us. God doesn't love us because of what we do or who we are, but because He is Love. The Bible says, ***"The one who does not love does not know God, for God is love"*** *(1 John 4:8).*

GOD IS HOLY AND JUST

While God is a God of love, God is also holy and just and therefore He must punish sin. The scriptures say ***"God… will by no means clear the guilty"*** *(Ex. 34:7b).*

How would you feel if someone stole everything you had and a judge let that man go because he said he was sorry and that he would never do it again? Would that judge have been just? No, because the sin must be punished. God is more just than any earthly judge.

So, it appears that there is a dilemma. God is a God of Love and He created man to spend eternity with Him. But, man has sinned and can't get himself into heaven because sin can't be in heaven! God solved that dilemma by sending Jesus Christ into the world.

JESUS CHRIST *(In your opinion, who is Jesus Christ)?*

This a very important question! Let's look at why.

WHO HE IS - GOD AND MAN

In your opinion, who is Jesus Christ? The Bible teaches that Jesus Christ is God! The scriptures say ***"in the beginning was the Word, and the Word was with God, and the Word was God; and the Word was made flesh*** *(became a man)* ***and dwelt among us*** *(John 1:1, 14)."* ***"The Word"*** was another name for Jesus Christ. Let's substitute Jesus Christ for The Word. Then, the verses would read - ***"in the beginning was Jesus Christ and Jesus Christ was with God, and Jesus Christ was God; and Jesus Christ was made flesh and dwelt among us."*** You see, the Bible tells us that Jesus Christ is God and that He took on human form and dwelt among us.

JESUS CLAIMED TO BE GOD

Jesus got into a conversation with the Jews that involved Abraham. Even though Abraham lived several hundred years before Jesus, Jesus said that Abraham rejoiced to see His day. The Jews mockingly wanted to know how Jesus could have possibly seen Abraham. Jesus replied ***"truly. truly. I say to you, before Abraham, I Am."*** They picked up stones to stone Him for blasphemy because they knew He had claimed to be the ***"I AM."*** That was the name that God had given to Moses when He asked God for His name. *John 8:51, 56, 58*

Jesus said, ***"I am the way and the truth and the life: no one comes to the father but through Me"*** *(John 14:6)*. Bold statement, wasn't it? Jesus was saying that to get to heaven, you had to go through Him!

Someone once said that Jesus claimed to be God. Either He was or He wasn't. If He wasn't, He was either a liar because He knew He wasn't, or He really thought He was God, making Him a lunatic. Because Jesus claimed to be God, there are only those three choices - He was either a liar, a lunatic, or God!

JESUS FORGAVE PEOPLE FOR THEIR SINS

Who can forgive someone for their sins against another unless they are God? Jesus was forgiving people for their sins. *(Matt. 9:2)*.

JESUS ACCEPTED WORSHIP

John 20:28 says ***"and Thomas answered and said to Him, 'my Lord and my God!"*** Jesus accepted that worship. He didn't say "Thomas, I'm not God!"

THE DISCIPLES BELIEVED JESUS WAS GOD

The disciples spent three years with Jesus and believed He was God. They proved that by going to their deaths for Him.

WHY DID GOD COME TO EARTH AND BECOME A MAN?

He loved us enough to come to earth and pay for our sins, so we could go to heaven. Here is a fictional illustration by pastor Jerry Mitchell.

FICTIONAL ILLUSTRATION ABOUT A VIKING KING!

When the Vikings terrorized the seas, there arose a great leader. He was wise, strong, just, and cared for his people. Early in his reign someone began stealing from the treasury. The King made a decree throughout the nation that the person caught stealing would receive ten lashes with a whip. No one was caught, so the king put forth a second decree for twenty lashes. Again no one confessed, nor was anyone caught. Finally, the King put forth a decree of fifty lashes for the person responsible for the thefts. Fifty lashes was very harsh punishment that no one had ever been given, and there was considerable doubt whether anyone could survive such a punishment.

They finally caught the guilty person, and do you know who it was? It was the Viking king's mother. Now the king loved his mother very much and was deeply grieved over her actions. However, he was also a just king who knew evil must be punished. The king was faced with an apparently unsolvable contradiction. Would his love allow his mother to go free or his justice allow the lashes which would mean almost certain death?

The entire nation came to see what their king would do. The king said "guilty" and ordered his mother to be tied to the stake in front of everyone. Just before the first lash was given, the king took off his royal robes, stepped behind his mother, and took the lashes on his own back. Therefore, he satisfied his love for his mother by protecting her from the punishment she deserved, and his justice, which demanded the sentence be carried out against the guilty party.

In this same way, God has satisfied His love for us personally, and His justice, by sending His Son Jesus Christ into the world to pay the price for our sins and to demonstrate God's love for us. Jesus accepted the punishment that we deserved which made it possible for us to be free from the load and guilt of our sin. The Bible says that ***"He made Him who knew no sin to be sin on our behalf, so that we might become the righteousness of God in Him"*** *(2 Cor 5:21).*

Jesus came back to life conquering the power of death, thereby making it possible for us to have spiritual life in heaven with God. He rose from the grave and many saw him after His death. The fact that many saw Him after His death was more proof that Jesus was and is God. It also freed the way for you and me to have eternal life in heaven.

WHAT JESUS CHRIST DID - By His death, He paid for our sins and by His physical resurrection, He assured us of being in heaven with Him, if we receive His gift of eternal life through faith.

FAITH

IS NOT - ***Temporary nor Is It a Mere Intellectual Belief***

Remember the verse that said, " ***for it is by grace you have been saved, through faith?"*** Many people think that they have saving faith that will get them into heaven, but they really don't know what true saving faith is. Let's see what true saving faith is not.

Knowing the facts that Jesus lived, died, and rose again from the grave is not saving faith. It is just an intellectual assent to certain historical facts. The Bible says ***"You believe that God is one. You do well; the demons also believe, and shudder"*** *(James 2:19)*. So, you see, intellectual belief alone isn't enough to save you. Satan and his demons know the facts.

People may trust God in things such as getting through a surgery, having a safe trip, or for financial situations. This is a good faith to have but it will not save you. Those things are temporary! They are all things of this life and have no eternal consequences.

So, what is true saving faith?

It is - ***Trusting in Jesus Christ ALONE for our salvation***

True saving faith is trusting in Jesus Christ ALONE for our salvation - not what we have done. Jesus Christ did for us what we could not do for ourselves!

If I offered you my watch as a gift and you said - "I don't need your watch - I'll go buy my own," and you walked away without receiving it, you would be rejecting that gift. Likewise, many will not go to heaven because they refuse to receive God's gift of eternal life. They think they can buy their way into heaven.

Jesus said ***"Truly, truly, I say to you, he who believes has eternal life."*** *(John 6:47)*. That's true saving faith!

Now, look at your answers to the two questions that I asked you. What was your answer to "**What would you tell God if He asked you - "why should I let you into my Heaven?"** Who you were trusting in for your salvation? You or Jesus?

Here is the complete 1 John 5:13 verse ***"These things I have written to you who believe in the name of the Son of God, so that you may know that you have eternal life."***

CHAPTER 2

ARE YOU A CHRISITAN?

IS YOUR FAITH GENUINE?

Does Everything in The Last Chapter Make Sense to You?

LET'S REVIEW:

Do you understand that....

The Gospel message tells us that heaven is a free-gift that cannot be earned or deserved.

The Bible tells us that mankind has separated himself from a perfect Holy God through sin.

Since it only takes one sin to separate man from God, there is no way that he can save himself.

While God is loving and merciful and desires that we spend eternity with Him, His holiness and justice requires that sin be punished.

The punishment for sin is total separation from God, forever.

The good news is that God had a plan to solve the dilemma that we caused due to our sin!

He satisfied both His love for us and His justice at the cross by coming to earth in the person of Jesus Christ to pay the required penalty for our sin.

After He paid for our sin by dying on the cross, Christ arose from the grave.

Christ's physical resurrection assures us of being in heaven with Him, if we receive His gift of eternal life through ***TRUE*** saving faith.

True saving faith is trusting in Jesus Christ, **ALONE** for our salvation. It is not enough to know the facts about Christ or to trust God for temporary things that have no lasting consequences beyond our life on earth.

The free-gift of eternal life is in Jesus Christ.

Trusting in anything other than Christ for salvation is rejection of God's free-gift!

Okay, that's the Gospel! Do you remember those questions that I asked you earlier?

- **Question 1**: Do you know for certain that you are going to heaven?
- **Question 2:** What would you tell God if He asked you - "why should I let you into my heaven?"
- **Question 3**: In your opinion, who is Jesus Christ?

When someone truly receives Jesus Christ as their Lord and Savior, their heart changes. The things that we will discuss here give a strong indicator if a person is a true Christian or not. These are not works. They don't save you, but they are true in your life if you are saved. If a person's heart hasn't changed, they are only calling themselves a Christian. They may sincerely think they are saved, but they are not.

So, what things are necessary that prove whether a person's heart has changed, proving whether they are saved or not?

CLARIFICATION OF SALVATION

The Bible says, ***"But as many as received Him, to them gave He the power to become the children of God, even to them that believe on His name"*** *(John 1:12)*.

"Him" is Jesus Christ. This verse tells us that a person who receives Jesus Christ is a child of God. To become "***children of God***" is synonymous with becoming a Christian. A "true" Christian is saved and will spend eternity with God. This verse goes on to say that we can be saved by believing on the ***"name"*** of Jesus Christ! Again, James 2:19 says ***"You believe that God is one. You do well; the demons also believe, and shudder. "***

Satan and his demons believe that Jesus died and rose from the grave, but they aren't saved! Believing the facts won't save anyone but believing on His name will. If Satan believes in Jesus Christ, doesn't he believe on the name of Jesus Christ? The answer is NO! Let's look at what ***"believe on His name"*** means.

BELIEVING ON HIS NAME

We like to look up what our names mean for fun. In Bible times, a person's name was not just a personal label. Each name had a meaning which was understood to match the character - attributes of the person holding the name. In short, the name was the person!

God had many names in the Bible. No one name could represent all His attributes. When Isaiah spoke of ***"the name of God is coming"*** *(Isa 30:27)*, instead of "God is coming," he was speaking of God coming in the attributes of that particular name. In Ps. 79:9-10, when God acts for ***"His name's sake,"*** He is acting regarding His reputation.

When God selected names for others, either before or after they were born, He was fixing their nature. In Matt. 1:21, speaking of Mary, the Bible says, ***"and she shall call His name Jesus for he shall save his people from their sins."*** Mary was told to name her Son Jesus **because** He would save His people from their sins! "Jesus" means "God is Salvation" or "God is Savior." "Christ" means "The Anointed One of God" which was the "Messiah" to the Jews or "Lord and Master" to us.

To believe on the Name "Jesus Christ" is to truly believe in your heart that Jesus Christ is everything that His Name contains. He is God, the Savior, and Lord and Master. He is someone you can really trust because of His love displayed on the cross for you. If you really believe all of that, you will want Him to be in your life.

TRUE SAVING FAITH" IS GENERATED BY A HEART THAT....

ACKNOWLEDGES CHRIST AS GOD and PERSONAL SAVIOR

If you are a true Christian, you will acknowledge that Jesus Christ is God and your Personal Savior. This means you really do believe that you are a sinner in need of a Savior; you are separated from a perfect Holy God because of your sin; that **only Christ** can save you from eternal separation from God; and that He could do this because He is God and is without sin.

RECOGNIZES CHRIST AS LORD and MASTER

Another thing a true Christian does is to recognize Jesus Christ as Lord and Master. This means that His will is more important to you than you own will and desires.

Imagine that you just got a new job. It is your desire to clock in and sleep half the day under your desk. Better yet, the boss can just mail you your check and let you stay home! But it is your boss's desire that you work for your paycheck. Whose will are you going to obey? Your boss's will is more important to you than your own will because he is in charge, kind of like a lord and master.

Imagine you are driving in the vehicle of your life, trying to find heaven. Jesus is in the passenger seat! As you try to find the way, you drive down a "dead end" street. You change direction, only to find yourself driving down another dead-end street. Finally, realizing you don't know how to find heaven, your destination, you stop the vehicle, get out from behind the wheel and ask Jesus to do the driving. You tell Jesus you will go willingly, anywhere He drives. Guess what! You are no longer lost! Jesus knows how to get there! He is from there! We need to turn control of our lives over to Jesus. So, how do we turn the wheel of our life over to Christ, so He can take control?

There is a map showing you how to get to heaven. The map is the Bible which is God's Word! We must desire to follow the Bible and obey whatever it tells us. If it contradicts what you want, you have two choices:

You can either say, "C'mon, everyone does that! I'll just keep doing what I'm doing, at least for now." Or, you can say to God that "even though I don't understand why this is wrong, I trust You and will stop." You relinquish your own will and follow His will. Prov. 3:5-6 says, ***"trust in the LORD with all your heart and lean not on your own understanding; in all your ways acknowledge Him, and he***

will make your paths straight."

The point is that a real Christian accepts God's will even if it is not what they think they want! And, the more we let Jesus take control of our lives, the more we grow to be like Him! That's because we will be doing what He wants.

It is also important to know that we are saved to worship and glorify God. Jesus said in John 14:15, ***"If you love Me, you will keep My commandments."*** He didn't say, "If you want to get to Heaven, keep My commandments." Again, we are not saved based on living a good life. A true Christian's life reflects what they really believe, otherwise, they are a hypocrite. And, if a person is rebellious, and doesn't' keep His commandments, they don't love Christ and are not accepting Christ as Lord and Master. Remember, Christ means Lord and Master!

By being obedient to Christ as Lord and Master and trusting Him to know best in all aspects of your life, your faith will grow as you see Him work in your life.

The point is that the best way to be a part of God's plan is to read the Bible and be obedient to it. A true saving faith is one that is lived out. Others need to see that you believe so that they will want Him in their lives too. The more we let Christ take charge of our life, the more we will grow to be like Him.

DESIRE TO REPENT OF *(TURN FROM)* SIN

Now, there are things that keep us from being like Christ. Those things are sin. God hates sin because there is no sin in God, and sin separated man from a perfect relationship with Him. He loved us enough to send His Son to the cross to pay the penalty for our sin and restore the relationship that we were created for.

So, if God hates sin, we should, also. Removing sin from our lives should be the desire of our heart. We will continue to sin - however, sin should no longer be the pattern of our life. The Bible says, ***"if we confess our sins, He is faithful and just to forgive us our sins and to cleanse us from all unrighteousness"*** *(1 John 1:9).* We need to admit to God that what we have done is sin.

I loved my dad. He died from cancer. Could I love my dad and the cancer that killed him? How could we say we love Jesus Christ and love the sin that sent Him to the cross?

Remember, we are saved by God's grace. Paul said – ***"What shall we say then? Are we to continue in sin so that***

grace may increase? May it never be! How shall we who died to sin still live in it" *(Rom 6:1-2)*?

We need to ask God to help us overcome the sin in our lives so that we can be more like Christ and show people we believe. Otherwise, we are hypocrites and people will not see our changed lives. If we think we can sin all we want because we are saved, we should examine our faith and question if we really are saved. Remember, Jesus is Lord and Master as well as Savior.

TRANSFERS TRUST TO JESUS

We must stop trusting in ourselves and our own good deeds. We must put complete trust in Christ to take control of our lives as well as our salvation. Since He is perfect, He can do a much better job of directing our lives than we can.

RECEIVES CHRIST INTO YOUR LIFE

Open your heart to Him and you will be saved - **IF** you are receiving Christ as God, Savior, Lord and Master and desire to worship and glorify God through a changed life.

If what has been shared here is new to you and you now believe it, you can receive the gift of eternal life right now.

But first, do you acknowledge that Christ is God and the only One who can save? Do you recognize Christ as Lord and Master? Are you ready to transfer all trust to Jesus Christ, alone? Is it the desire of your heart to repent of your sins? Then are you ready to receive Christ into your life?

The next page is a chart representing the entire gospel

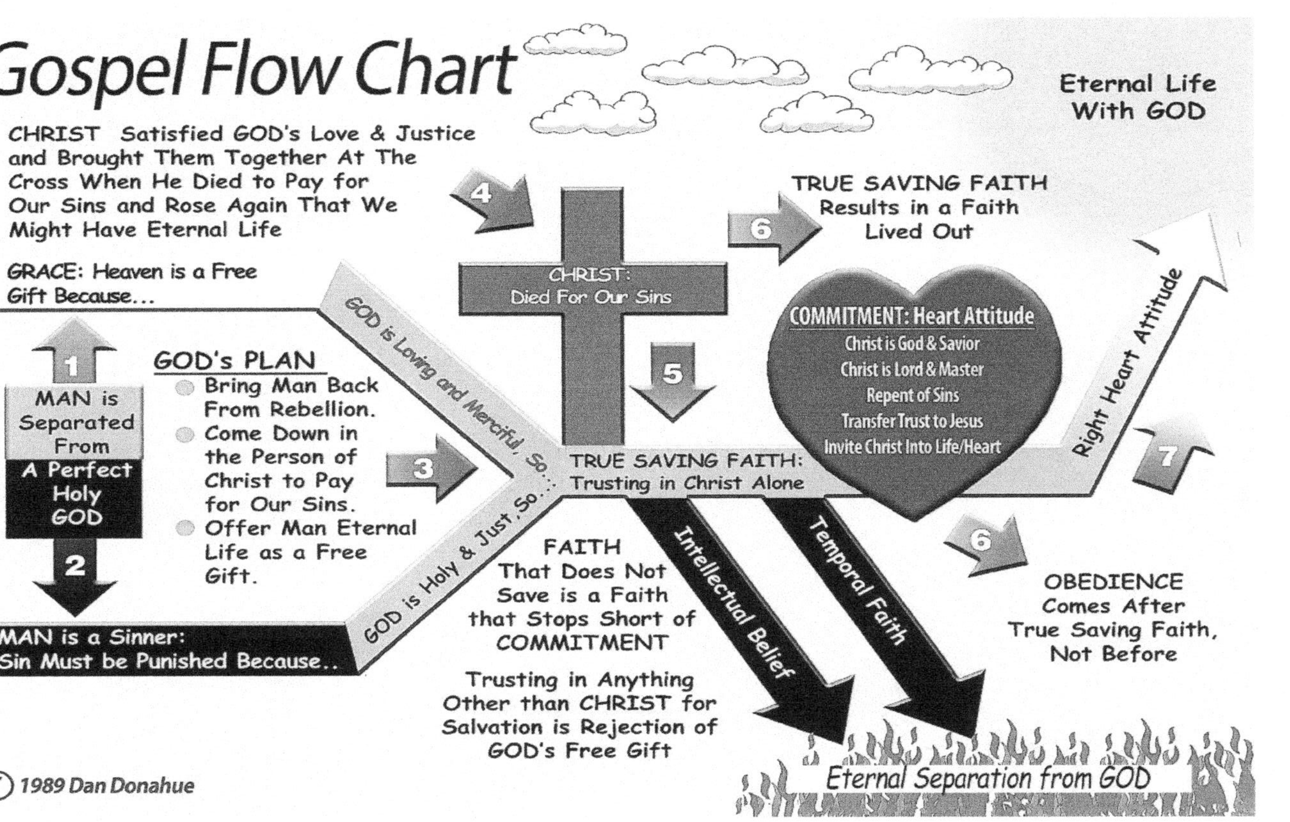
Gospel Flow Chart
CHRIST Satisfied GOD's Love & Justice and Brought Them Together At The Cross When He Died to Pay for Our Sins and Rose Again That We Might Have Eternal Life
GRACE: Heaven is a Free Gift Because...
1
MAN is Separated From
A Perfect Holy GOD
2
MAN is a Sinner: Sin Must be Punished Because..
GOD's PLAN
Bring Man Back From Rebellion.
Come Down in the Person of Christ to Pay for Our Sins.
Offer Man Eternal Life as a Free Gift.
GOD is Loving and Merciful, So...
GOD is Holy & Just, So...
3
4
CHRIST: Died For Our Sins
5
6
TRUE SAVING FAITH Results in a Faith Lived Out
TRUE SAVING FAITH: Trusting in Christ Alone
COMMITMENT: Heart Attitude
Christ is God & Savior
Christ is Lord & Master
Repent of Sins
Transfer Trust to Jesus
Invite Christ Into Life/Heart
Right Heart Attitude
7
Eternal Life With GOD
6
OBEDIENCE Comes After True Saving Faith, Not Before
Intellectual Belief
Temporal Faith
FAITH That Does Not Save is a Faith that Stops Short of COMMITMENT
Trusting in Anything Other than CHRIST for Salvation is Rejection of GOD's Free Gift
Eternal Separation from GOD
© 1989 Dan Donahue

CHAPTER 3

DO YOU WANT TO RECEIVE JESUS CHRIST INTO YOUR LIFE?

PRAYING TO RECEIVE CHRIST AS SAVIOR AND LORD AND MASTER OF YOUR LIFE.

If you agree with and believe what has been shared so far and you realize that you need and desire to have God in your life, you can pray about this right now.

However, please don't pray to receive Christ if you don't mean it. God knows our hearts. Words are not magic. To be saved, your heart must be right. The words you pray should be an expression of your heart. The prayer will not accomplish anything unless you are sincere. If you still desire to receive Christ into your life, it will result in giving up your life style to follow Christ. Knowing that, do you still want to receive Christ? If you do, here is a sample prayer.

"Lord Jesus, I want You to come into my life right now. I am a sinner. I have been trusting in myself, but now I put my trust in You. I accept You as my personal Savior. I believe You died for me. I receive You as Lord and Master over my life. Help me to turn from my sins and follow You. I accept Your gift of eternal life. In your name, I pray, Amen."

ASSURANCE OF SALVATION

If you really meant that prayer or a similar prayer in your heart, then you will spend eternity with God. This is a relationship that can never be broken or reversed. In other words, once you are saved by trusting in Jesus Christ alone for your salvation, you can never lose your salvation. If you can't earn your way into heaven by works - then, you can't lose your salvation because that would be based on the lack of works which is still works!

Here are just a few of the many verses that will give you assurance that you cannot lose your salvation.

Jesus said, ***"Most assuredly, I say to you, he who believes in Me has everlasting life"*** John 6:47. Do you believe? If so, you have eternal life with God in heaven.

"As far as the east is from the west, so far has He removed our transgressions from us" Psalm 103:12. How far is the east from the west?

"And the testimony is this, that God has given us eternal life, and this life is in His Son. He who has the Son

has the life; he who does not have the Son of God does not have the life" 1 John 5:11-12. If you are in Jesus, you have eternal life because He has eternal life.

"Therefore, if anyone is in Christ, he is a new creature; the old things passed away; behold, new things have come" 2 Corinthians 5:17.

"Therefore, there is now no condemnation for those who are in Christ Jesus" Romans 8:1. If you are saved, you can't be condemned - go to hell.

ASK YOURSELF THESE QUESTIONS ONE MORE TIME.

Question 1: Do you know for certain that you are going to heaven?

Question 2: What would you tell God if He asked you - "why should I let you into my heaven?"

Question 3: In your opinion, who is Jesus Christ?

Who are you trusting in now?

CHAPTER 4

GROWING IN YOUR FAITH

When you are saved *(become a Christian)*, there are things that will help you grow in your faith.

READ and STUDY THE BIBLE

God communicates with us through His Word, the Bible. Read it and study it. This is God's living Word to us. This is how God instructs, encourages, strengthens, and comforts us. You might want to start by reading John and 1 John. Even if you start by reading one chapter a day you will grow.

If you see verses that mean a lot to you, memorize the Scripture. As Christians, we need to have God's Word in our hearts. Memorizing Scripture is the way to keep God's Word close to you always. Two other verses that show the value of memorizing God's Word are Joshua 1:8 and Psalm 119:11.

"This book of the law shall not depart from your mouth, but you shall meditate on it day and night, so that you may be careful to do according to all that is written in

it; for then you will make your way prosperous, and then you will have success" Joshua 1:8.

"Your word I have treasured in my heart, That I may not sin against You" Psalms 119:8.

PRAY TO GOD, FOR OTHERS, and FOR YOURSELF

God communicates with us through His Word, and we communicate with God through prayer. As a child of God, you now have a "direct line" to the Father. Just like you share with people every day, make it a habit to start your day with God. Here are some Bible verses that talk about prayer: 1 Thessalonians 5:16-18 and Philippians 4:6-8.

"Rejoice always; pray without ceasing; in everything give thanks; for this is God's will for you in Christ Jesus." 1 Thessalonians 5:16-18.

"Be anxious for nothing, but in everything by prayer and supplication with thanksgiving let your requests be made known to God. And the peace of God, which surpasses all comprehension, will guard your hearts and your minds in Christ Jesus. Finally, brethren, whatever is true, whatever is honorable, whatever is right, whatever is pure, whatever is lovely, whatever is of good repute, if there

is any excellence and if anything worthy of praise, dwell on these things" Philippians 4:6-8.

WITNESSING TO OTHERS FOR GOD

As mentioned before, God desires for us to tell others about our new life in Christ. Just share what has happened with those you know. There's also another way you can tell people what you've done. That's through baptism. The Bible shows the pattern for this in the book of Acts, the record of the early church. The Bible states that those who believed in Jesus Christ were baptized as a further expression of their belief. *(Acts 2:41; 10:47).*

"So then, those who had received His word were baptized; and that day there were added about three thousand souls." Acts 2:41.

"Surely no one can refuse the water for these to be baptized who have received the Holy Spirit just as we did, can he?" 10:47

WORSHIP and FELLOWSHIP

Another part of your new life is belonging to a church family. We are all part of God's family and it is His desire that we fellowship with each other for encouragement and support. Hebrews 10:25 encourages us in this. Find a church that teaches the Word of God. Become involved there.

The Holy Spirit gives you gifts that are important to the local church. Fellowship with those in the family of God will bless you as you associate with other believers who can help you grow and pray for you. You will be used by God to help others grow.

SATAN

One last thing you need to know. Now that you've joined God's family, Satan is your enemy. He will try to create doubt in your mind and spoil God's work in you. Christ defeated Satan when He arose from the grave, but Satan will still try to defeat you. The only way we can be strong against him, or defeat his deceitfulness, is through knowing God's Word.

Ephesians chapter 6 shows you where our strength comes from. Notice verse ten that says, ***"Be strong in the Lord, and in the strength of His might."*** On our own, we are weak, but with God we are strong. We need to follow Christ's example when He was tempted by Satan *(Matthew*

4:1-11). Each time Satan came, Christ quoted Scripture. That's another good reason to memorize Scripture.

ONE ADDITIONAL NOTE ABOUT EXPANDING OUR FAITH

As mentioned before, God wants us to become more like Christ, which results in a closer relationship with Him. Then, we can be better used to glorify Him and lead others to Christ by our faith. One-way God expands our trust in Him is by stretching our faith in Him.

As an example, let us suppose that our faith is three inches wide. God will allow a set of circumstances in our life that requires four inches of faith. Since this is one inch outside our faith, it's just far enough outside our faith to stretch us but not break us. He knows how much we can handle.

We may get worried and try to work out the situation, we are in, by ourselves. This is due to a lack of faith or trust that God can handle the situation. We might not even think of Him. Then, when all else fails, we will turn to God. We'll get down on our knees and ask Him to handle the situation. When He does, our faith becomes four inches wide.

If all of life's circumstances were within our three inches of faith, we would never grow. This stretching process will continue all our life. The more we let Christ take charge of our life, the more we will grow to be like Him. Then, He will be revealed to others, through us, bringing glory to Him and salvation to others.

The best way to be a part of God's plan is to read the Bible and be obedient to it. A true saving faith is one that is lived out. Realizing that something in my life that tests my faith might just be that - a test to make my faith grow. Have faith in God in all situations.

CHAPTER 5

GOD'S ATTRIBUTES
Revealed to Me in My Life

WHAT GOD HAS SHOWN ME ABOUT HIMSELF IN MY LIFE

In my first book, "Beyond Coincidence: Things that only God could have done in my life," I gave personal testimony of how I was taken from demonic possession to salvation and many other personal stories, proving that God is alive and at work giving proof of what you have just read. I can say with certainty that there were and are no coincidences in our lives.

God had **complete control** over what happened and is happening in my life. Of that, there is no doubt.

In my experiences, God has proven to me that **He is a personal Spirit**, who is **always present**.

He **hears my prayers and answers them**, whether over a long or short period of time. Sometimes He answered in seconds, and sometimes, He had to prepare me to accept what I prayed for. He controlled what happened in my past and is continuing to do so. Sometimes His answer is "no." He knows what is best for us better than we do.

He even **guided me** to events that caused me to pray for something, even before I had prayed for it. He is **all-knowing**.

He demonstrated that He can allow something seemingly bad to happen in my life and turn it to my good. That is **total power, love**, and **complete control**. As stated, He allowed me to experience total darkness, which I caused, to guide me to the light - into a personal relationship with Him, proving that He is **sovereign** over everything.

He didn't have to save me from harm, but He did. He had **patience** with me and revealed His **love, grace, and mercy** to me. That gives me faith and hope for the future. He set things in motion before I asked Him to, to give me eternal life. He has never let me down, so He is a **God of truth**. I can always trust Him because He says I can.

If you are His child, don't worry about anything. If you make what you think is a mistake, Scripture tells us that *"God causes all things to work together for good to those who love God, to those who are called according to His purpose"* Rom 8:28. He turns bad, and seemingly mistakes, into good for His children.

He proved these things about Himself to me. If you don't know Him, He can prove it to you. If you don't know God, ask Him to show you the truth. That's what I did. Get to know Him. Let Him show you His love, grace and mercy.

PART TWO

SHARING
About
ETERNAL LIFE

CHAPTER 6

SHARING YOUR FAITH WITH OTHERS

In Part One, we briefly discussed telling others about your new relationship with Jesus Christ. That also relates to older believers as well as new believers.

John MacArthur said that ***"the greatest form of worship is to share Christ with others!"***

"If you know where you will spend eternity and realize the horror of not spending it with God, you should want to share your faith with others. You will want your loved ones to spend eternity with you and a loving God. You will not want them to suffer the consequences of not doing so. The dread situation of not going to heaven will, and with the prodding of the Holy Spirit, even make you concerned about the eternal destiny of strangers. First, let's look at how to handle determining someone's relationship with Jesus Christ.

THOSE TWO QUESTIONS

To help determine someone's spiritual condition, it's a good idea to ask the two questions that were asked in chapter one. Here is how to analyze the answers you receive.

QUESTION ONE: Do you know for certain you are going to *heaven?*

This will be a "yes" or "no" answer. If someone says, "I hope so" or "I think so," or "I don't think anyone can know for sure," their answer was "no" they aren't certain. That is when you quote 1 John 5:13 - ***"These things I have written to you....so that you may know you have eternal life."*** This verse says that a person can know.

QUESTION TWO: How would you answer God if He asked you, *"why should I let you into My heaven?"*

Sometimes, it can be difficult to interpret their answer to this question. Their answer may sound good, but not be a clear - faith in Jesus Christ answer. If the answer is vague, you may need to dig deeper. Vague is when you still don't know if they are trusting Jesus Christ alone for their salvation or trusting in themselves.

If I'm still not sure who they are trusting in for their salvation after hearing their answer, a good follow-up question that works most of the time for me, is, "what would you tell your children or friends if they asked you how to become a Christian?" I usually get a clear answer here if I don't get it by asking them what they would say to God. Maybe they don't want to admit to others, particularly people they are close to, that they don't know how to get to heaven.

So, why not start with asking the question of how they would answer friends? Asking them what they would say to God is very personal and you don't usually get a "learned" answer.

What to look for when given an answer to that question - do they say, "because I" or "because Jesus?" Let me illustrate this for you by sharing an actual conversation I had.

EXAMPLE OF INTERPRETING WHAT IS BEING SAID

I was training two people how to share their faith. We visited someone who they knew, and thought was saved. We asked him if he knew for certain that he would go to heaven. He said "*yes - I was a sinner and I was in a bad car wreck and God saved me.*" We asked him why God should let him into heaven. He said, "*because I am repenting of my sins.*"

The team thought those were good answers. I wanted to press on a little because I still had some doubt. I knew he had a daughter, so I asked him what he would say to her if she ever asked him how she could become a Christian. He said "*I would tell her to obey the 10 Commandments because that is the prerequisite for getting into heaven (his exact words).* "

The people with me could not believe his answer because they knew him and were sure he was saved. I shared the Gospel with him. At the end, he said - "*I'm not saved!*" He realized it himself. He prayed to receive Christ.

I explained to the people who knew him that God saved him from the auto accident and his idea of repenting of his sins was cleaning up his life by works (earning his way to heaven by becoming a better person). He prayed to receive Christ when he realized this.

I use this example because it demonstrates that sometimes you need to probe to find out where that person is spiritually. Again, this is my basic test - is the person saying "I" or is he saying "Christ?" "I received

Christ as my Savior" may be a good answer - but even that is what he did. What did Christ do? Just ask him what he meant by that answer.

Watch for cliché answers. I visited a man who said he should go to heaven because "he believed on the name of Jesus." I asked him what that meant. He admitted he didn't know. He had heard someone say it and thought that's what we wanted to hear.

Sometimes we will never know what a person's spiritual status really is. But we can get a good idea most of the time.

Oh, sometimes you will get an "I don't know" to the first question and a faith answer to the second question. They might be a believer who has lost the assurance of their salvation - maybe because of sin in their life, or they feel that they are not doing anything for Christ. That results in losing their joy in Christ. These have been some of my favorite visits because hearing the Gospel again can get them excited again and their life for Christ gets back on track.

CHAPTER 7

FEAR OF SHARING CHRIST WITH OTHERS AND THE SACRIFICE IT MAY REQUIRE

Many are afraid to share what Jesus did for them. They may try to reason that they aren't an evangelist, so sharing is best left to the professional. The very thought of sharing makes them feel uncomfortable.

However, Eph 2:10 says, ***"For we are His workmanship, created in Christ Jesus for good works, which God prepared beforehand so that we would walk in them."*** He did create us to reveal Himself to others. Sometimes, it will cost us. The works mentioned in this verse are not to save us but come after we are saved.

Phil 1:29 says, ***"For to you it has been granted for Christ's sake, not only to believe in Him, but also to suffer for His sake."*** We will suffer for Christ's sake, which can be uncomfortable. So, is being uncomfortable really so bad? Jesus stated clearly what it means to follow Him. Jesus ***"was saying to them all, "If anyone wishes to come after Me, he must deny himself, and take up his cross daily and follow Me. For whoever wishes to save his life will***

lose it, but whoever loses his life for My sake, he is the one who will save it." (Luke 9:23-25).

The fear for many comes from not being able to articulate what they believe; or they are afraid someone might ask a question they can't answer; or they are afraid that their friends and relatives might reject them; or they are trusting in their own power and their own resources which they know to be lacking. That is scary isn't it! Well, if you don't feel adequate - good!

2 Cor 3:5 says ***"Not that we are adequate in ourselves to consider anything as coming from ourselves, but our adequacy is from God."*** We aren't supposed to feel adequate in ourselves! You don't need to fear, if you trust God! **Isa 41:10** says- ***"Fear thou not: for I am thy God; I will strengthen thee; I will uphold thee with the right hand of My righteousness."***

Only God can save! Saving is His ministry and He is looking for someone to use who realizes that they cannot share Christ in their own power. He wants believers to make themselves available and trust in His abilities to work through them. Don't put someone's destiny on yourself. If you share and trust Him, that's all you can do.

If you are scared, step out in faith and make yourself available to be used by Him. He will not put a desire to glorify Him in your heart and leave you to fail in your own power! He is an all-powerful God! When you are not in your comfort zone, turn yourself over to God, and you will see amazing things happen. Just make yourself available. I get most excited when it's obvious that God is working. When you experience this, your faith deepens, and your joy increases because, during this process, you are experiencing God.

Again, if we want to **experience** God in our life, it will take sacrificing our time or whatever is holding us back and to step out of our comfort zones. I attended a class by Henry Blackaby that made things very simple.

Henry Blackaby says that there are **"Seven Realities"** to **"Experiencing God."** **(1)** ***God is always at work around you;*** **(2) He wants a personal relationship with you,** so that **(3)** ***you will become involved with Him in His work***. So, how do we know what work He wants us involved in?

(4) ***God speaks to us by the Holy Spirit and through the Bible*** telling us what He wants us to be involved in. However, **(5)** ***Working with Him always***

leads you to a crisis of belief that requires faith and action, and, **(6)** ***you must make major adjustments in your life to join God in what He is doing.***

You can't serve God by staying in your comfort zone! In short, **(7)** ***you come to experience God as you obey Him and He accomplishes His work through you."***

So, when we come to our crisis of belief it is because we are focused on our own abilities! We need to turn the work over to Him and trust in His abilities. Then, we'll experience God as He works through us to do the things that we know we can't do on our own. David said that he would not offer to the Lord that which cost him nothing *(1st Chronicles 21:24).* Henry Blackaby says that ***"Any true ministry for God is going to cost you something or it is not a ministry for God!"***

Don't worry about fear or sacrifice! God doesn't ask you to do something and not give you the resources to accomplish it. Experience the purpose that you were created for. Join God by making yourself available to share Christ with others.

SHARING WITH YOUR HEART

Don't worry about how skilled you think you need to be in order to share Christ with others. If you have love and concern for the lost souls of the world, God will use you. Here is an example of how the Lord can use you.

The following example is from the book "Effective Evangelism" by J. O. Sanders.

"I went to hear D.L. Moody preach when I was a country minister and he so fired my heart that I went back to my country church and tried to preach as he preached, and we had really a great work of grace. It did not start immediately, and I was so discouraged, because things did not go as I thought they ought, that I called my church officers together and said: 'You will have to help me.'

They promised to do so and finally an old farmer rose and said: 'I have not done much work in the church, but I will help you.' One of the officers said to me afterwards: 'Do not ask him to pray, for he cannot pray in public,' and another said: 'Do not ask him to speak, for he cannot speak to the edification of the people.'

Next morning, we had one of those sudden snowstorms for which that part of the country is famous, and this old farmer rose and put his horse to his sleigh and started across the country four miles to a blacksmith's shop.

He hitched his horse on the outside and went into the shop all covered with snow and found the blacksmith alone. The blacksmith said: 'Mr. Crammer, whatever brings you out today?' The old farmer walked to the blacksmith's bench, and putting his hands upon the man's shoulders, said: 'Tom, when your old father died, he gave you and your brother into my guardianship, and I have let you both grow to manhood and never asked you to be a Christian.'

That was all. He did not ask him then; he could not. He got into his sleigh and drove back home. And he did not go out again for months; he almost died from pneumonia.

But that night in the meeting, the blacksmith stood up before my church officers and said: 'Friends, I have never been moved by a sermon in my life, but when my old friend stood before me this morning with tears and sobs, having come all through the storm, I thought it was time I considered the matter.' We received him into the Church, and he is a respected church officer today. Preaching fails, singing fails, but individual concern does not fail"

"If I speak with the tongues of men and angels, but do not have love, I have become a noisy gong or a clanging cymbal" (1 Cor 13:1).

Make yourself available to be used by God and watch what happens.

CHAPTER 8

WRAP-UP

OUR MOTIVES

We have talked about how we can become a Christian. But, how does someone know for sure that they are one? We will not get to heaven by anything we do. No one can be good enough or do enough. That includes going to church, walking down an aisle, reading the Bible, or praying a prayer, if we are not sincere.

God knows our hearts and if we are trusting doing those things to please Him so we can get to heaven. Likewise, He knows if we are truly accepting Jesus Christ as our Savior because we realize we can do absolutely nothing on our own to get there. So, don't even pray a prayer to be saved unless you mean it. Instead, pray for understanding.

Consider Proverbs 2:1-6 as it says, ***"my son, if you accept My words and store up My commands within you, turning your ear to wisdom and applying your heart to understanding — indeed, if you call out for insight and cry aloud for understanding, and if you***

look for it as for silver and search for it as for hidden treasure, then you will understand the fear of the LORD and find the knowledge of God. for the LORD gives wisdom; from his mouth come knowledge and understanding."

RECAPPING GOD'S PLAN OF SALVATION

First, let's review what we need to believe to get to heaven – the gospel.

- The gospel message tells us that heaven is a free gift that cann***ot*** be earned or deserved.
- The Bible tells us that man has separated himself from a perfect Holy God through sin.
- Since it only takes one sin to separate man from God, it's impossible for him to save himself.
- While God is loving and merciful and desires that we spend eternity with Him, His holiness and justice requires that sin be punished.
- The punishment for sin means total separation from God, forever.
- The good news is that God had a plan to solve the

dilemma that we caused through sin!

- He satisfied both His love for us and His justice at the cross by coming to earth in the person of Jesus Christ to pay the required penalty for our sin.
- After He paid for our sin by dying on the cross, Christ arose from the grave.
- Christ's physical resurrection assures us of being in heaven with Him, if we receive His gift of eternal life through ***true*** saving faith.
- True saving faith is trusting in ***Jesus Christ, alone*** for our salvation. It is not enough to know the facts about Christ or to trust God in for temporary things that has no lasting consequences beyond our life on earth.
- The free gift of eternal life is in Jesus Christ.
- Jesus said there was no other way to heaven but through Him. ***"I am the way and the truth and the life: no one comes to the father but through Me"*** *(John 14:6)*.
- Trusting in anything other than Christ for salvation is rejection of God's free gift!

Second, because He loved us enough to die a gruesome death for us on a cross and made it possible for us to spend eternity in heaven with Him instead of hell, we should be willing to make sacrifices to share His love with others.

Others need to know of His sacrifice to have a chance of receiving Jesus Christ as their personal Savior and Lord and Master so they can enter heaven also.

Rom 10:17 says, ***"faith comes from hearing, and hearing by the word of Christ."***

A person comes to **faith** only through **hearing** the gospel, and the specific message that must be heard is the **Word of Christ**, that is, the good news about Jesus Christ as the crucified and risen Savior.

This book was intended to give a clear message of the gospel, to encourage those who do not know the way of salvation to receive Jesus Christ as their Savior and Lord, and to encourage those who are thankful for their salvation to share that good news with others.

So, step out in faith and go share what Jesus has done for you! To God be the glory!

770-222-7733

Made in the USA
Monee, IL
18 February 2021

59882936R00046